THE
READING
HOUSE

This book belongs to:

Text copyright © 2022 Caterpillar Books Ltd.
Cover art and interior illustrations copyright © 2021, 2022 by WeDoo Studio
All rights reserved. Published in the United States by The Reading House,
an imprint of Random House Children's Books, a division of
Penguin Random House LLC, New York. The Reading House and
the colophon are registered trademarks of Penguin Random House LLC.
rhcbooks.com
Educators and librarians, for a variety of teaching tools,
visit us at RHTeachersLibrarians.com
ISBN: 978-0-593-51615-7
Printed in China
10 9 8 7 6 5 4 3 2 1
First North American Edition
CPB/1800/2031/1121

Kindergarten Basic Skills

Contents

This is going to be **fun**!

Welcome to The Reading House

Marla Conn, MS Ed., is a reading and literacy specialist with a Master of Science in Elementary Education and Reading, and over 15 years of experience as a teacher in New York public schools.

During my years as a teacher, literacy specialist, and educational consultant, I have worked with hundreds of children and have a deep understanding of how the right books and instructional materials can provide rich, meaningful experiences that build a strong foundation for learning.

The Reading House was created out of the need to provide children with a comprehensive and systematic educational tool. It combines dependable strategies that have been proven to motivate, educate, and spark the process of learning, using an innovative storybook, character-based approach.

What began as a leveled learn-to-read program has grown into an entire educational universe, with materials to cover all aspects of early learning, in a variety of engaging formats. Each book in the series has been carefully devised and designed to inspire and encourage young children and adheres to the core principles and key building blocks of early learning.

Let's get **started**!

The Reading House is one-of-a-kind: an inviting, accessible, informative space where children can learn and grow. With its engaging cast of characters, bright and playful illustrations, and consistent setting, The Reading House is a world that early learners will love to return to, again and again.

I am so excited for children to get their hands on these books and to watch the lightbulbs switch on!

Happy Reading!
Marla Conn

Hints and Tips for Parents and Guardians

Kindergarten Basic Skills supports kindergarteners in the development of the overarching early learning skills and concepts they will need to be school-ready. Designed to be as enjoyable as it is educational, little learners are joined on their journey by the fantastically fun cast of The Reading House.

The activities in this workbook build upon the basic preschool concepts learned in **My First Learning Skills**, introducing children to a more complex set of skills, including reading and writing, developing math, basic science, everyday skills, and social studies. This workbook is the perfect companion for readying learners for their school ventures.

Before embarking on this exciting journey, there are a few hints and tips parents and guardians should bear in mind.

☆ BUILD SKILLS:

This workbook has five main sections: reading and writing; math; science; everyday skills; and social studies. These sections can be approached in any order, but ideally material within each section should be followed in order for a progressive development of skills. Children can supplement their learning with the accompanying **Kindergarten Reading and Writing** and **Kindergarten Math** workbooks in this series.

☆ HELP:

As you progress through the workbook with your child, help them by reading instructions aloud and explaining activities further.

☆ ANSWERS:

Refer to the answers section at the back of the workbook once your child has completed an activity. Ensure they fully comprehend the concept presented before moving on to the next activity.

☆ WRITING INSTRUMENT AND GRASP:

By kindergarten age, your child is getting comfortable using a pencil as their hand muscles and fine motor skills are developing. It is helpful, however, to frequently reinforce ideal pencil grasp, per the following steps:

We love learning in **Happy Town!**

- Hold the pencil between thumb and index finger, with index finger on top.

- Rest the pencil on the middle finger.

- Rest the side of the hand comfortably on the table.

☆ FORMATION:

This workbook uses a system of dots and numbered arrows to demonstrate the correct formation of characters.

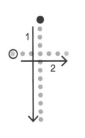

- ● The black dot indicates the starting point for the pencil.

- → The arrows show the direction of pencil movement, and should be followed in numerical order.

- ◎ This additional dot indicates that the pencil should lift off the page to make a separate stroke.

☆ WRITING LINES:

This workbook uses writing lines consisting of three lines with a dotted center to encourage proper character formation.

Tracing Aa to Zz

Trace the **uppercase** and **lowercase letters** of the alphabet.

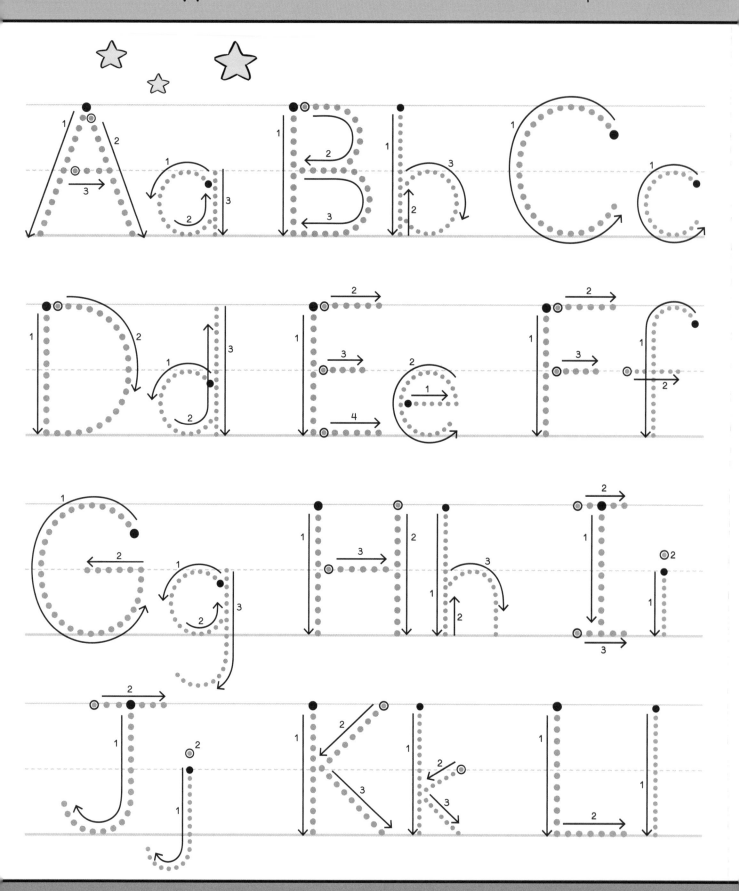

Writing Aa to Zz

Now **write** the **uppercase** and **lowercase** letters one by one, using the pictures as clues.

Beginning Sounds

Write the lowercase letter for the sound these words **begin** with.

oo

og

ey

nt

gg

us

Middle Sounds

Match each picture to the correct word and **middle** sound.

tub

map

hog

pig

hen

a

e

i

o

u

The letters a, e, i, o, and u are called **vowels**. They're really useful letters!

End Sounds

Circle the correct **end** sound of the picture and write it in the space.

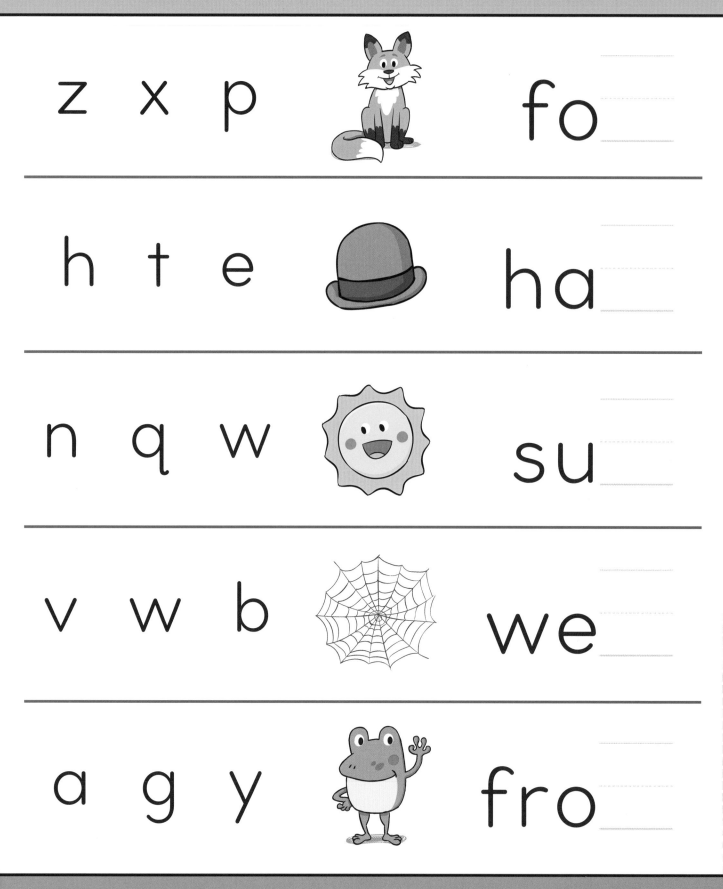

z   x   p   fo____

h   t   e   ha____

n   q   w   su____

v   w   b   we____

a   g   y   fro____

Word Scramble

Unscramble the **letters** and write the **words** out correctly.

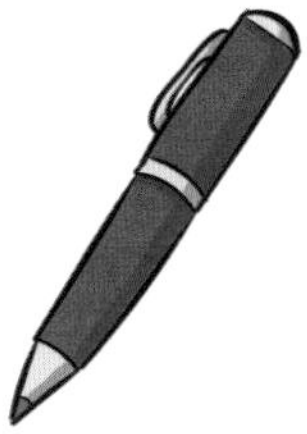

e n p

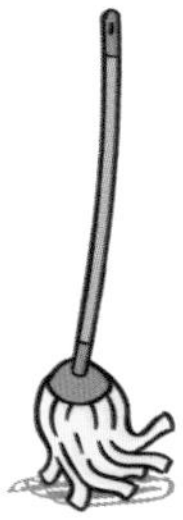

o p m

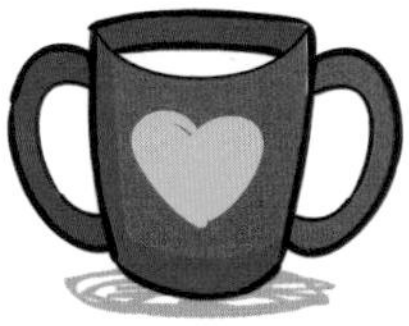

p c u

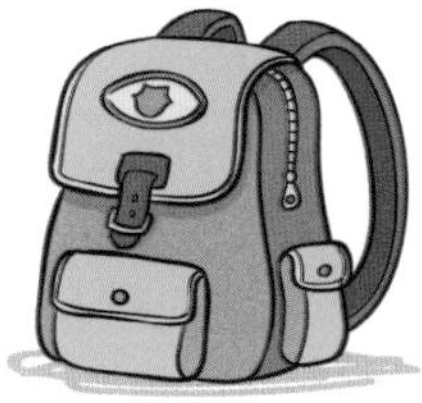

g a b

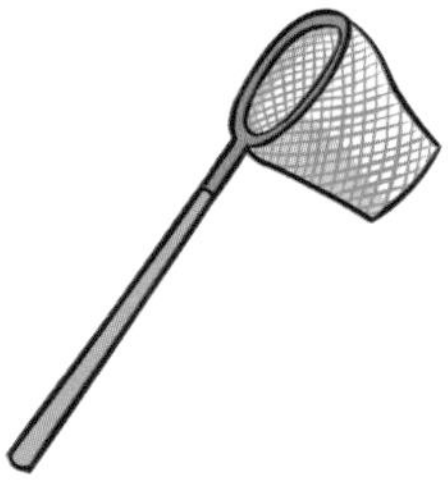

e n t

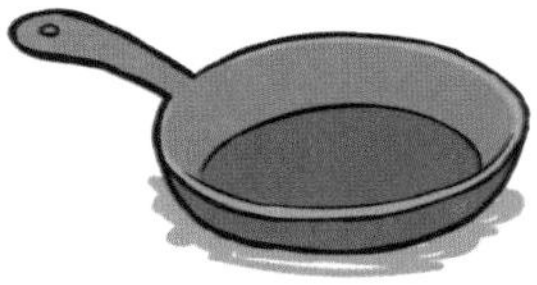

n p a

Rhymes

Words that make the **same vowel end sound** are **rhymes**. Say the words out loud and circle the word that **rhymes** with the first in each row.

cat	hat	bug	box
van	log	pen	pan
pig	bug	cup	dig
dog	log	box	hop

hen	hat	bug	pen
mop	pan	hop	box
rug	bug	pen	cup
fox	log	hat	box
up	cup	pan	dig

Sight Words Match

Draw lines to pair the matching **sight words**.

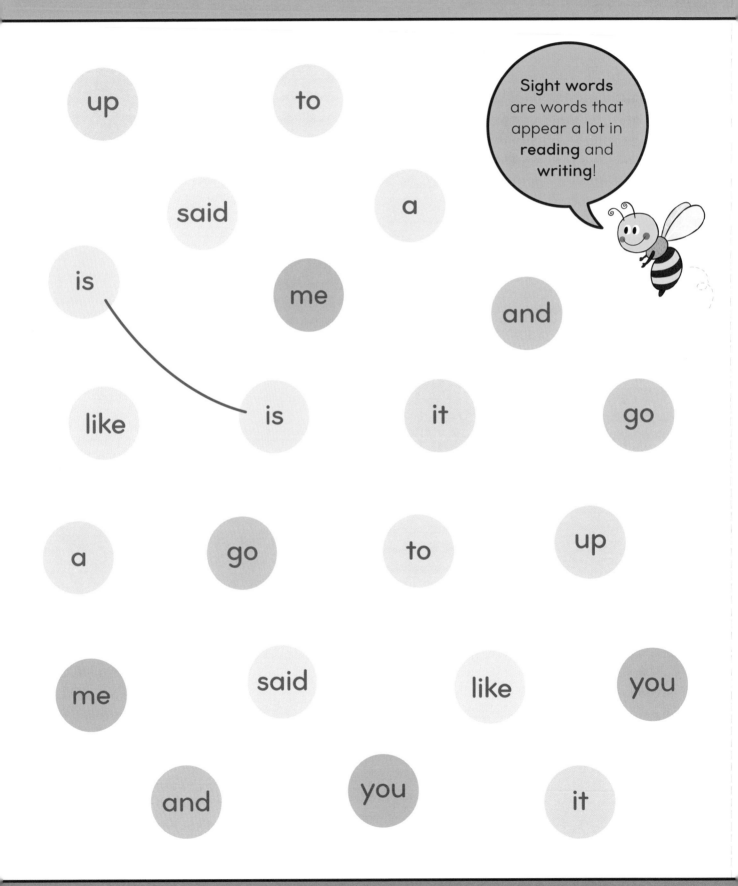

up

to

said

a

Sight words are words that appear a lot in **reading** and **writing**!

is

me

and

like

is

it

go

a

go

to

up

me

said

like

you

and

you

it

Sight Word Search

Find and circle the **sight words** in the word search.

we	too	big	for	so
do	my	all	come	the
in	be	can	here	are
am	by	see	on	at

a x k o s d b g z t

l f o r e c e i e h

l t v x e k o t g e

s o c a n j h m y o

j n w k m q d v e e

i v y i m t i e d o

r b r h e r e r r w

g a r e v e a t x e

Color Sight Words

Trace and write the **color sight words**.

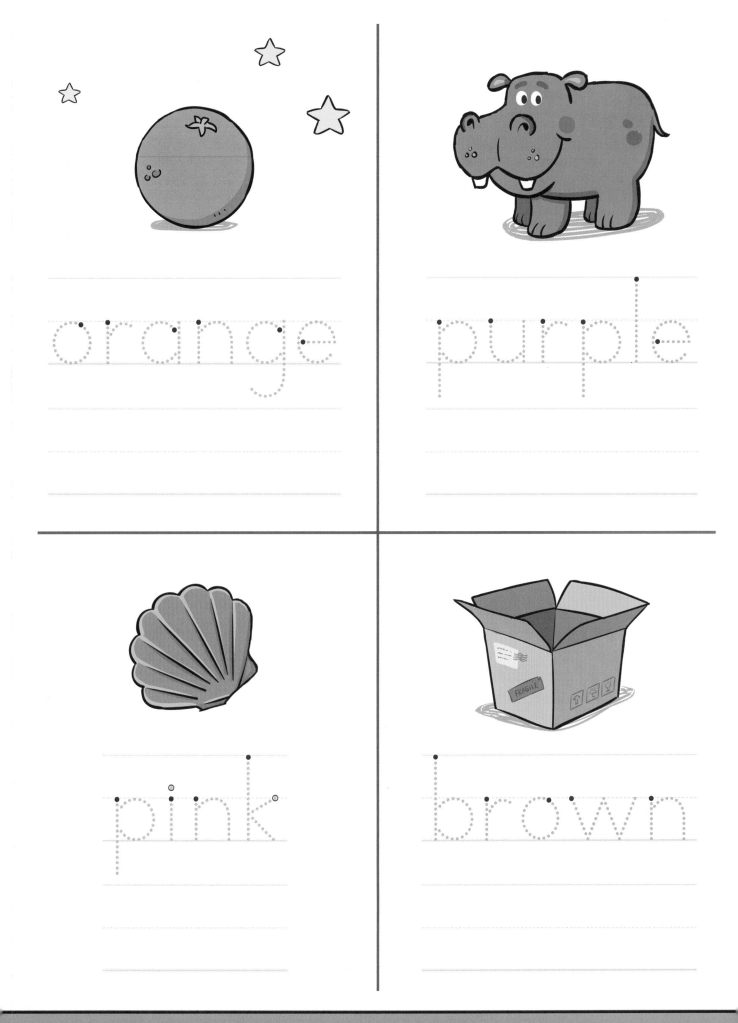

orange

purple

pink

brown

Count the Beat

A **syllable** is a beat in a word. Say each word out loud and count the number of syllables. Color a dot for every beat you count.

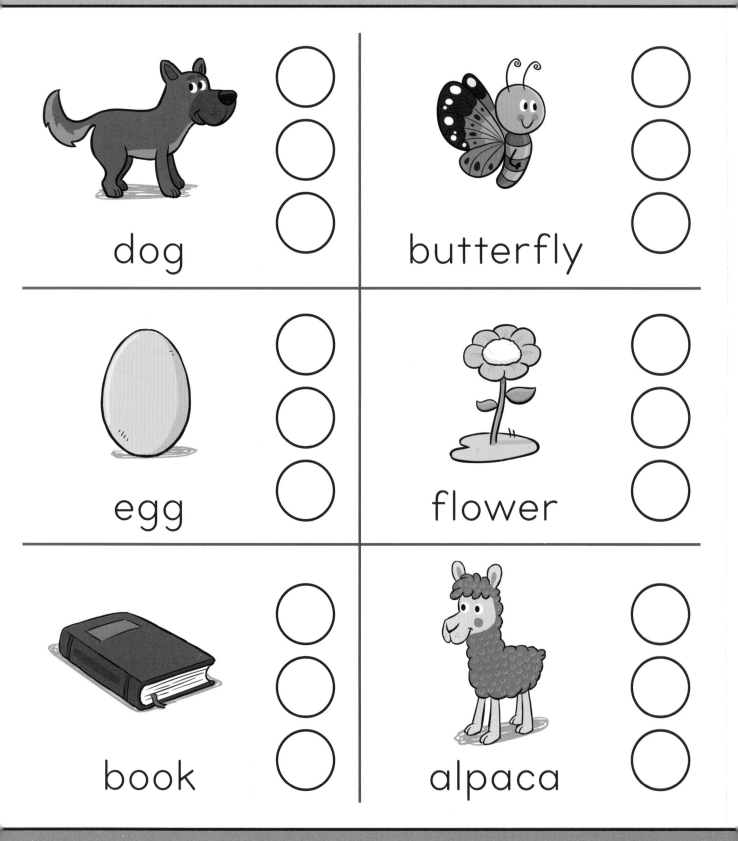

dog

butterfly

egg

flower

book

alpaca

Syllable Match

Count the **syllables** in each word, write the number, and then match the words that have the same number of syllables.

frog

unicorn

octopus

rabbit

zebra

box

Building a Sentence

A sentence contains **uppercase** letters, **lowercase** letters, **spaces**, and a **period**. All sentences need structure. Unscramble the words in each activity below to form **sentences**.

a / car. / Cat / drives

Dog / log. / on / is / the

book. / Bee / a / reads

goes / the / to / Lion / library.

Sequencing Events

Put these pictures in the correct order to tell a **story**, by labeling them with numbers I through 3. Number I is the **beginning** of the story, 2 is the **middle**, and 3 is the **end**.

2

3

I

Drawing a Story

Draw a made-up **story** here. Use the first box for the **beginning** of your story, the second box for the **middle**, and the third box for the **end**.

Questions to think about:

What happens in your story?

Who is in your story?

When does the story happen?

Where does the story happen?

Why do you like your story?

(1) Beginning

2 Middle

3 End

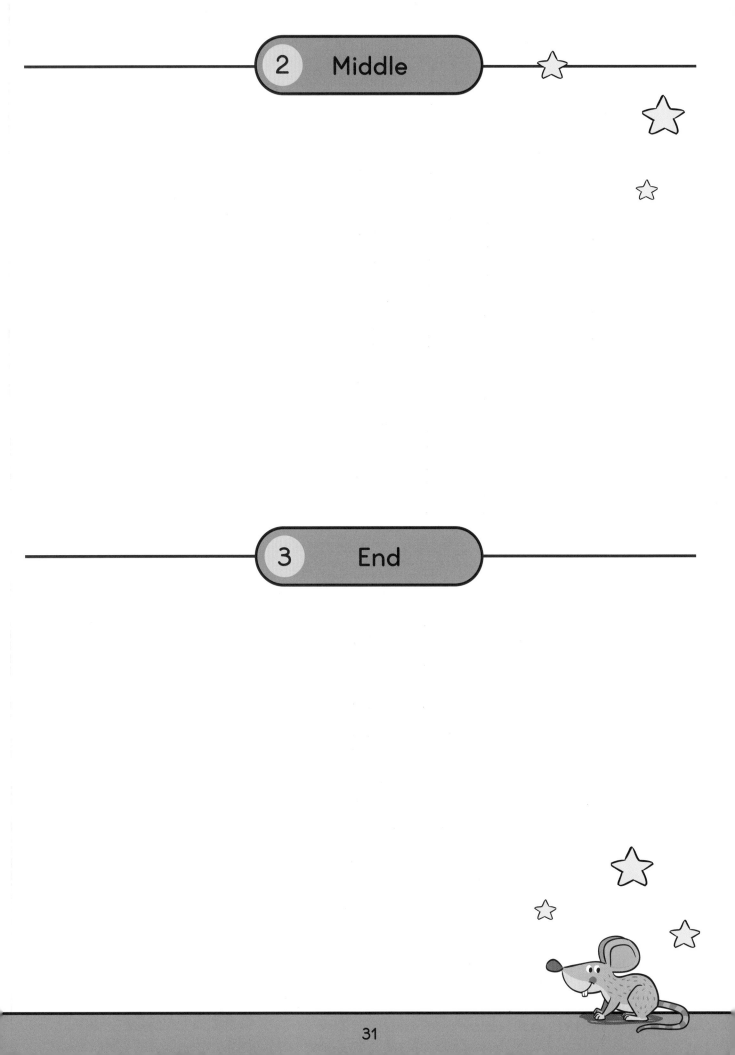

Number Practice

Count the objects and draw lines to match them to the **numerals** and **words**.

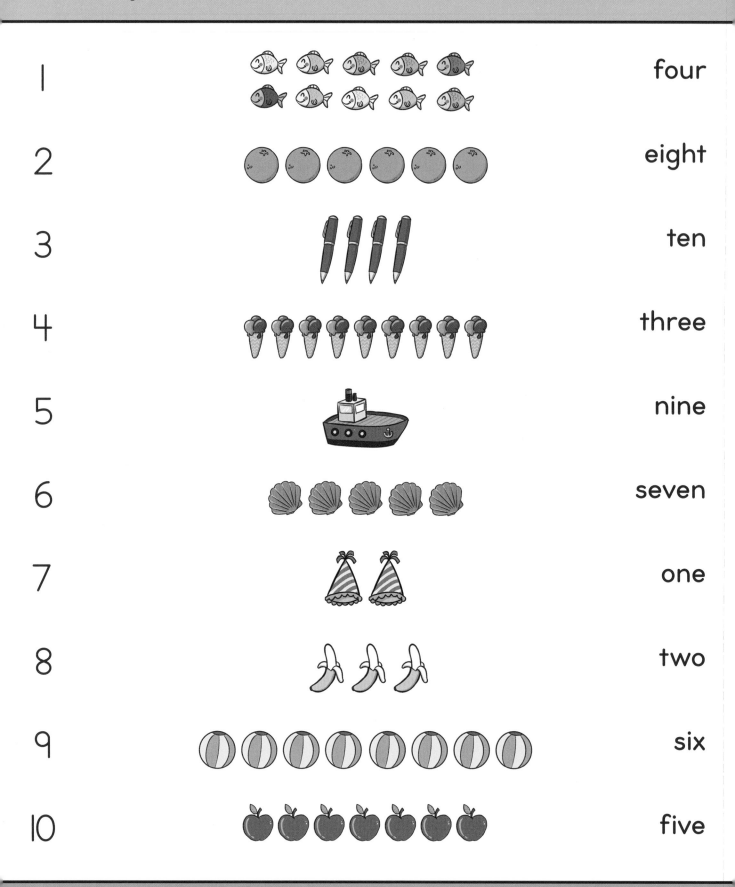

1		four
2		eight
3		ten
4		three
5		nine
6		seven
7		one
8		two
9		six
10		five

11		nineteen
12		fourteen
13		twenty
14		fifteen
15		seventeen
16		eleven
17		sixteen
18		twelve
19		eighteen
20		thirteen

Skip Counting

Look at the numbers in each **skip counting** pattern and write the number that comes next.

2   4   6   8

1   3   5   ___

5   10   15   ___

10   12   14   ___

Odd and Even

Circle each **pair** of objects and **write** the total number of objects.
Check the **odd** or **even** box.

If all the objects can be joined into pairs, the number is **even**. If there is an object without a pair, then the number is **odd**.

3

☐ even

☑ odd

☐ even

☐ odd

☐ even

☐ odd

☐ even

☐ odd

☐ even

☐ odd

Addition

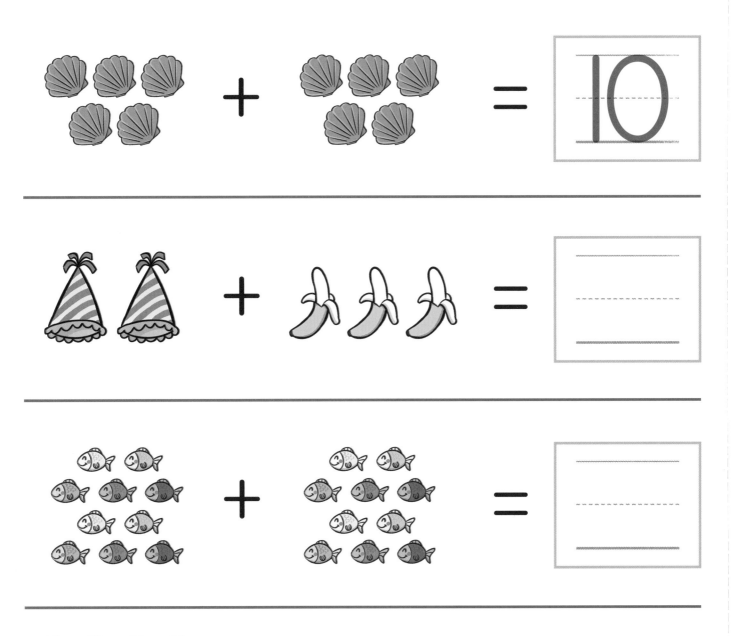

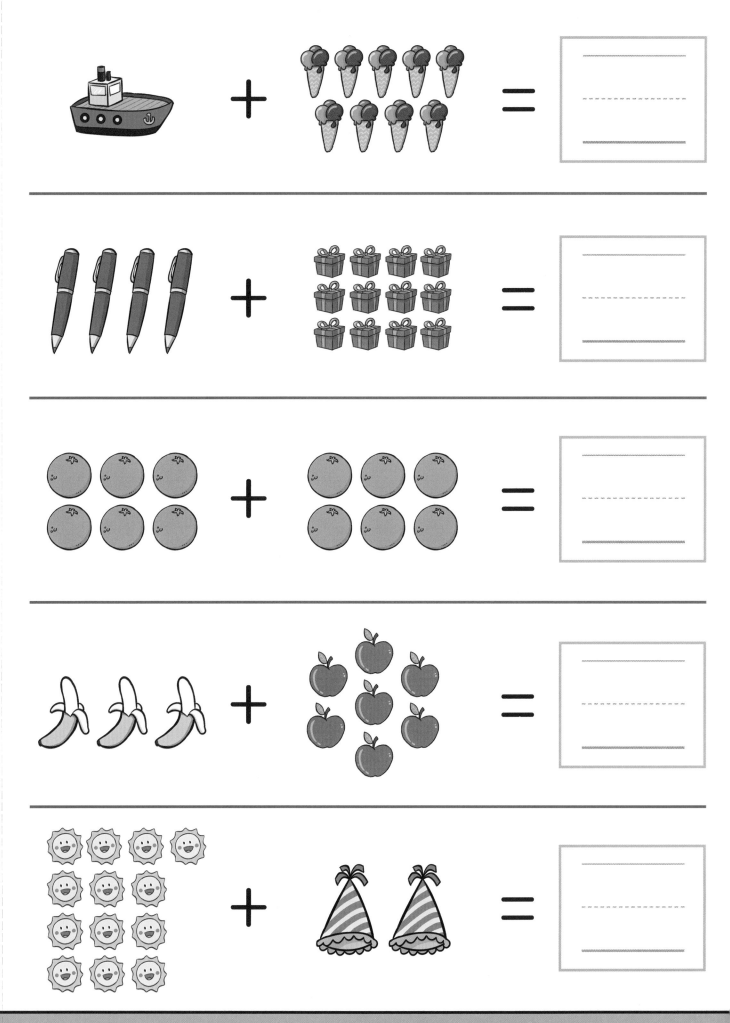

Subtraction

Count the objects on the left, and from that number, subtract the number of objects on the right.

If it helps, cross out numbers to see what is left over!

— = 1

— =

— =

— =

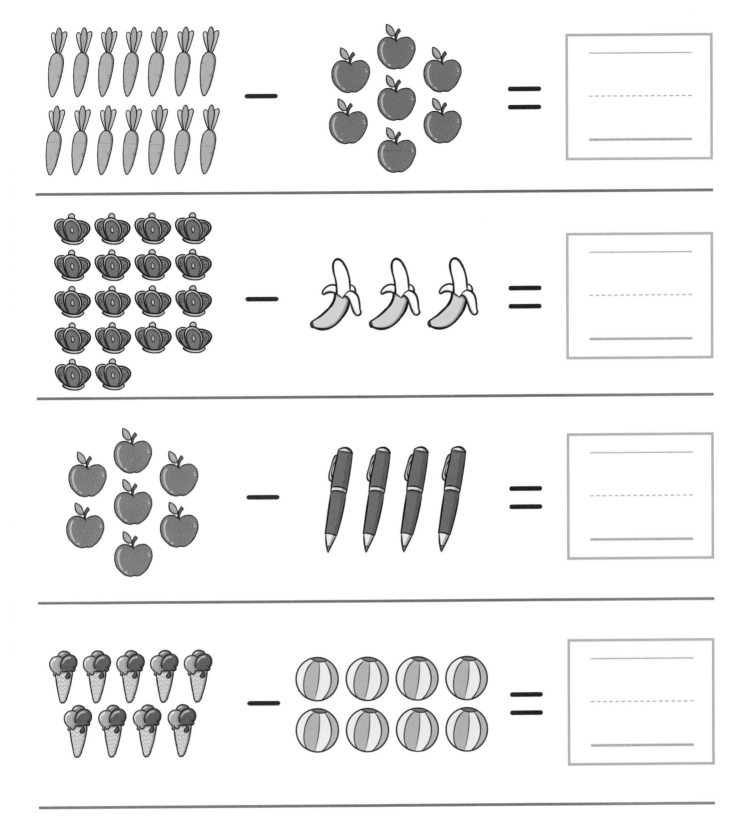

2D Shapes

Trace each **shape** and count its **corners** and **sides**.

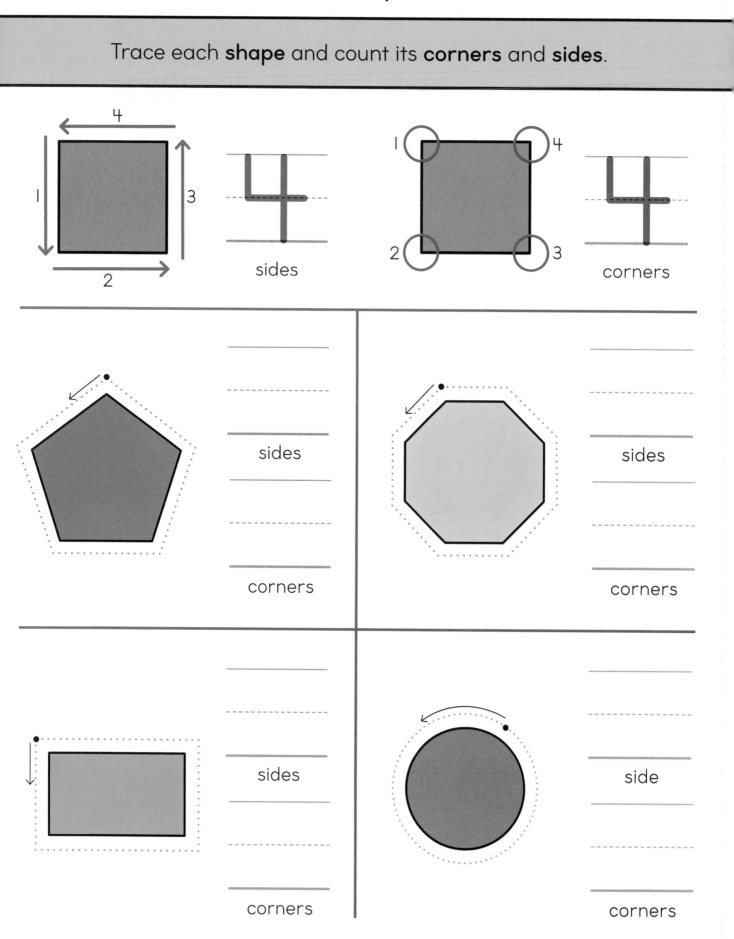

sides

corners

sides

corners

sides

corners

sides

corners

side

corners

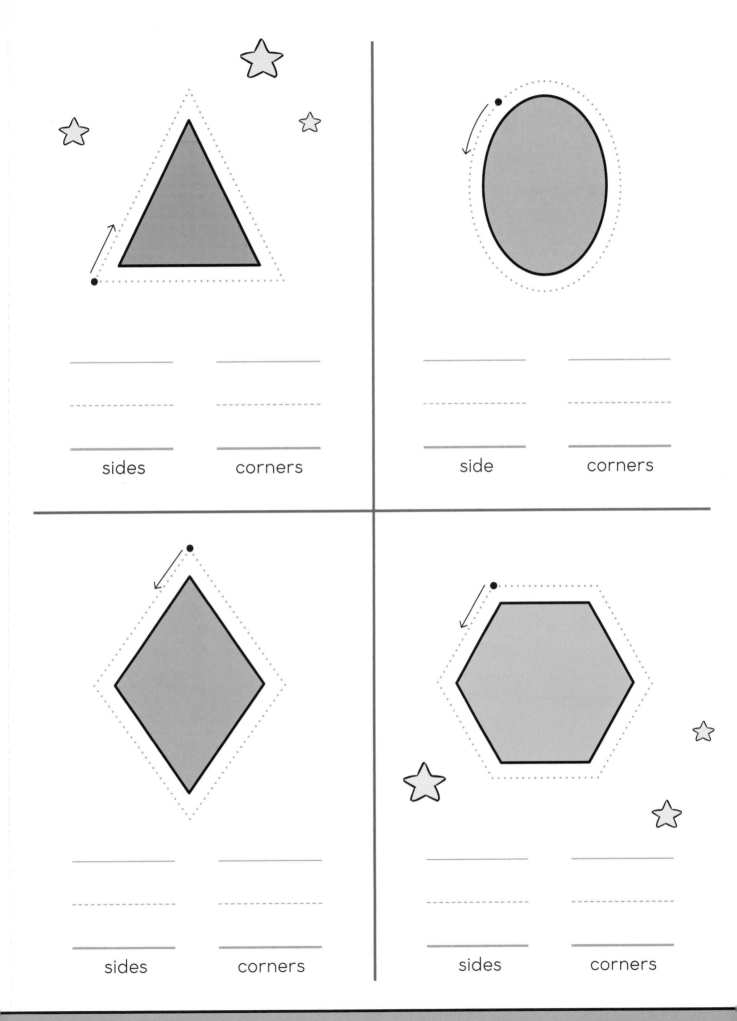

sides   corners

side   corners

sides   corners

sides   corners

3D Shapes

Color the **2D** shapes in blue and the **3D** shapes in red.
Then, draw them in the correct box on the next page.

octagon

cube

A 2D shape
is **flat**, whereas
a 3D shape
is **not flat**.

diamond

rectangle

cylinder

pyramid

cuboid

pentagon

square

oval

cone

hexagon

sphere

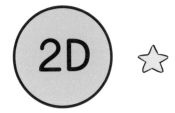

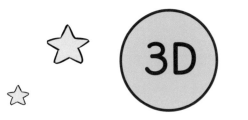

Identify and Sort

Look at each row of pictures and follow each **instruction**.

Circle the **fruits**.

Circle the **red objects**.

Circle the **triangles**.

Circle the **3D shapes**.

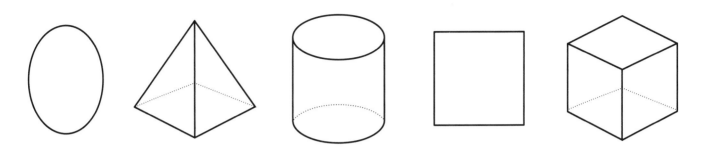

Circle the **odd one out**.

Circle the **yellow objects**.

Circle the **even numbers**.

Measure and Sort

Look at each row of pictures and follow each **instruction**.

Circle the **tallest** animal.

Circle the **heaviest** thing.

Circle the **shortest** animal.

Circle the **smallest** animal.

Circle the **longest** ruler.

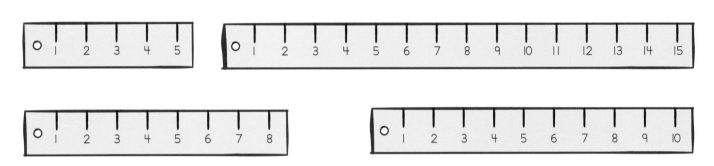

Circle the **biggest** animal.

Circle the **lightest** thing.

Living Things

Circle the pictures that show **living** things.

Animals, bugs, and plants are all **living things**.

Animal Food

Animal Habitats

Follow the lines to lead each animal **home**.

Butterfly's Life Cycle

Put these **life cycle stages** in the correct order, from numbers 1 to 4, with egg being the first stage.

egg

1

butterfly

caterpillar

cocoon

Plant Parts

Draw lines to match each label to
the correct part of the **plant**.

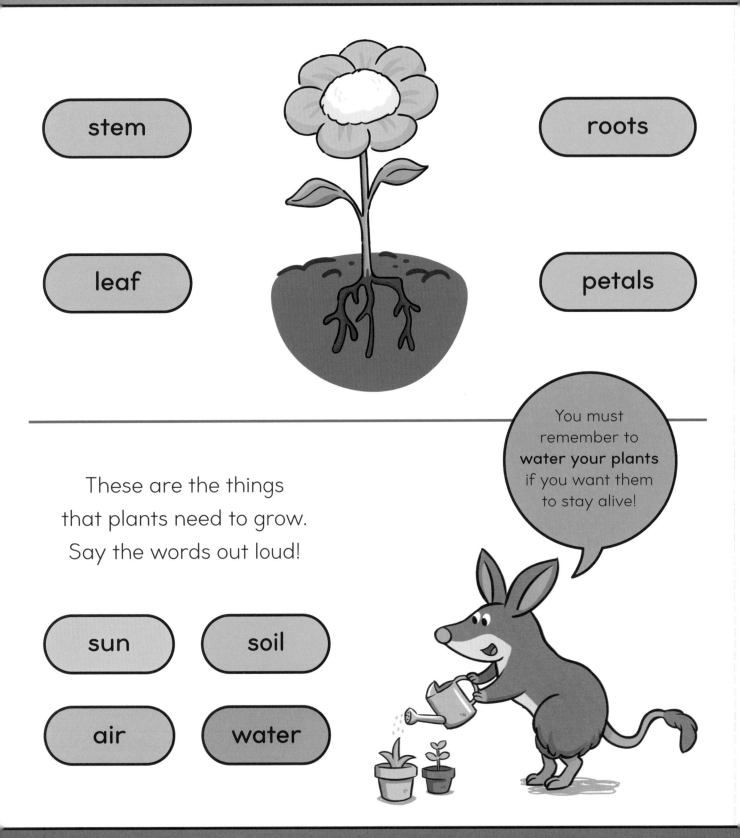

stem

roots

leaf

petals

These are the things
that plants need to grow.
Say the words out loud!

You must
remember to
water your plants
if you want them
to stay alive!

sun

soil

air

water

In the Garden

Put these stages of growing a **plant** in the correct order with number 1 being the first stage and 4 as the last.

plant

flower

sprout

seed

Seasons

Match the tree to the **season** in which it belongs.

spring

summer

fall

What is your favorite season?

winter

Weather

It's snowy

It's sunny

It's windy

It's rainy

Light and Dark

Match each object to its **shadow**.

When an object gets in the way of a source of light, like the **sun** or a **flashlight**, a **shadow** forms behind the object.

Hot and Cold

Is it **hot** or **cold**? Draw the
items in the correct box.

Hot

Cold

Solids and Liquids

A **solid** keeps its shape, while a **liquid** takes the shape of its container. Some things can turn from solid to liquid, and back again—like water!

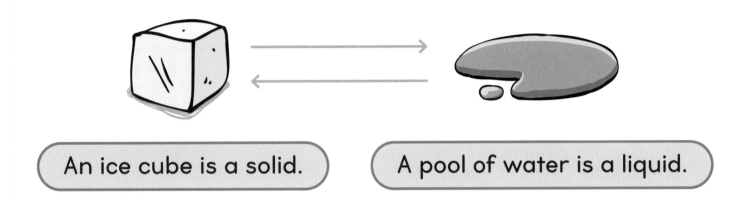

An ice cube is a solid.

A pool of water is a liquid.

Draw a **circle** around all the solids.
Draw a **square** around all the liquids.

rain

bell

juice

newspaper

pond

cake

ball

Tell the Time

Draw a line between the **clock** and the **time** it tells. The long blue hand shows the **minutes** and the short red hand shows the **hour**.

10 o'clock

6 o'clock

1 o'clock

4 o'clock

Draw the **clock** hands in the correct place.

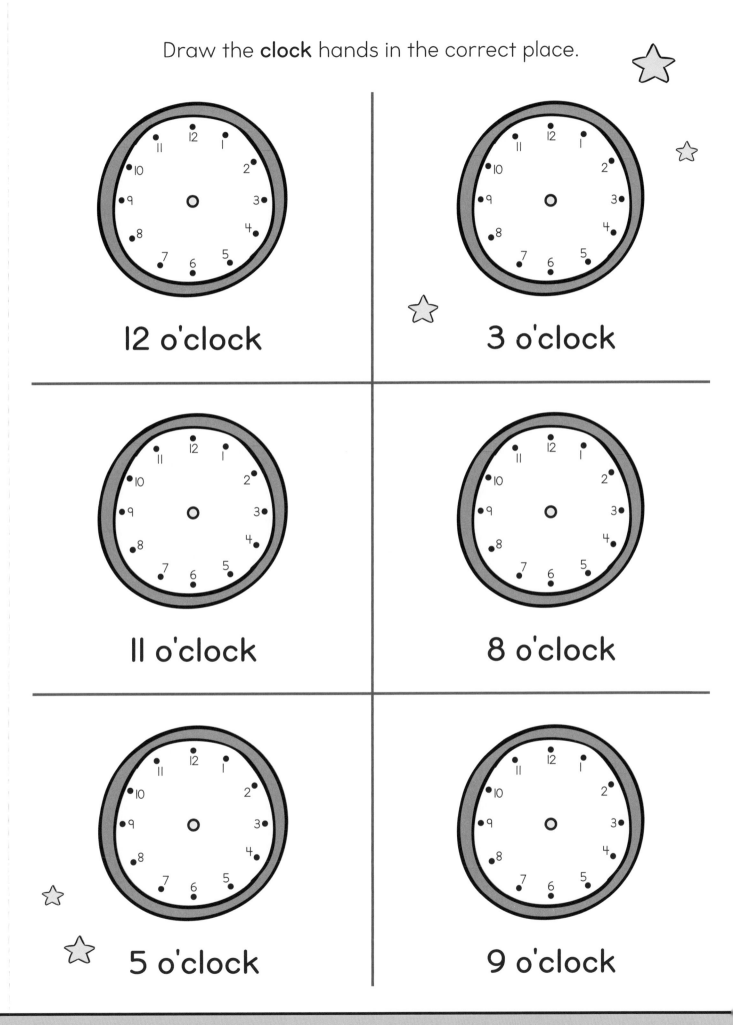

12 o'clock

3 o'clock

11 o'clock

8 o'clock

5 o'clock

9 o'clock

Times of Day

Color the **time of day** when the following activities happen.

Get home from school
- morning
- afternoon
- evening

Go to bed
- morning
- afternoon
- evening

Wake up
- morning
- afternoon
- evening

Eat breakfast
- morning
- afternoon
- evening

Take a bath
- morning
- afternoon
- evening

See the moon
- morning
- afternoon
- evening

Add times to the clock to show what **time** you do things during your normal day.

In the morning I...	In the afternoon I...	In the evening I...

...wake up at:

...eat lunch at:

...take a bath at:

...go to school at:

...get home from school at:

...go to bed at:

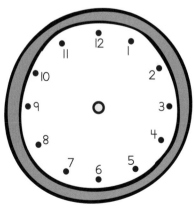

Days of the Week

These are all of the **days** of the **week**.

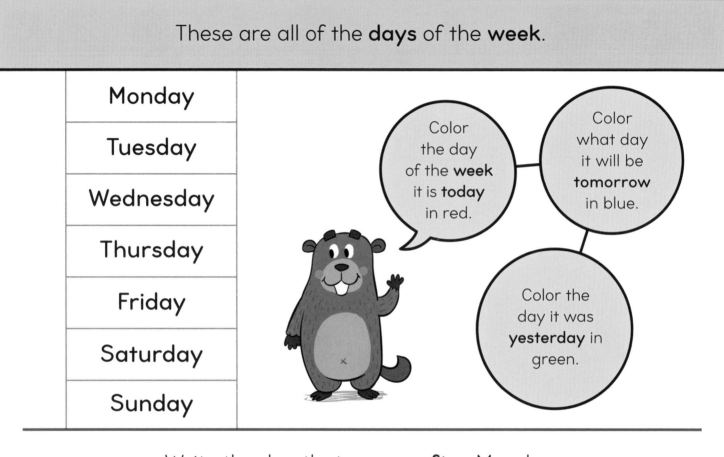

| Monday |
| Tuesday |
| Wednesday |
| Thursday |
| Friday |
| Saturday |
| Sunday |

Color the day of the **week** it is **today** in red.

Color what day it will be **tomorrow** in blue.

Color the day it was **yesterday** in green.

Write the day that comes **after** Monday.

Write the day that comes **before** Friday.

Write the day that comes **between** Tuesday and Thursday.

Months of the Year

Color which **month** it is now in yellow.

Color your **favorite** month in purple!

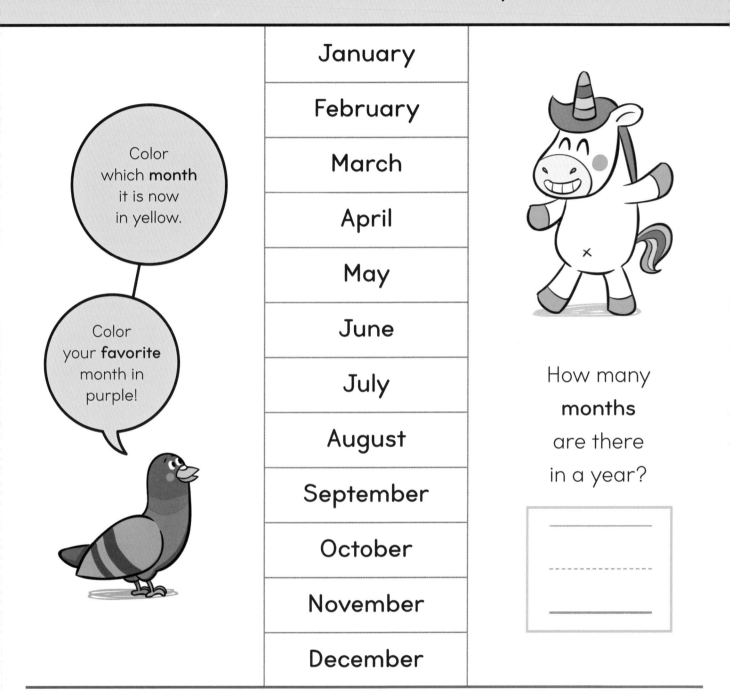

| January |
| February |
| March |
| April |
| May |
| June |
| July |
| August |
| September |
| October |
| November |
| December |

How many **months** are there in a year?

Write which month your **birthday** is in!

Healthy Foods

Separate the food into **healthy** food and **treats**, and draw them in the correct column. Draw a **star** around your **favorite** food.

Healthy	Treats

Time to Exercise

Circle the **activities** that help you to **exercise** your body.
What is your **favorite** way to exercise?

reading a book

jumping rope

running

playing catch

baking

swimming

sleeping

At the Shop

At the shop, you have to **pay** for the things you want.
Circle all the **coins** you will need to use to **pay** for each item.

nickel
5 cents

penny
I cent

dime
10 cents

| 10 cents | 21 cents | 25 cents |

Recycle!

Once you've finished using something, it's a great idea to **recycle**! Draw lines to match each item to the correct **recycling bin**.

Recycling is good for the **environment**!

PAPER   METAL   GLASS   PLASTIC

Happy Town

Cat is in the middle of **Happy Town**!

School

Park

Car wash

Library

Market

Beach

Shop

Zoo

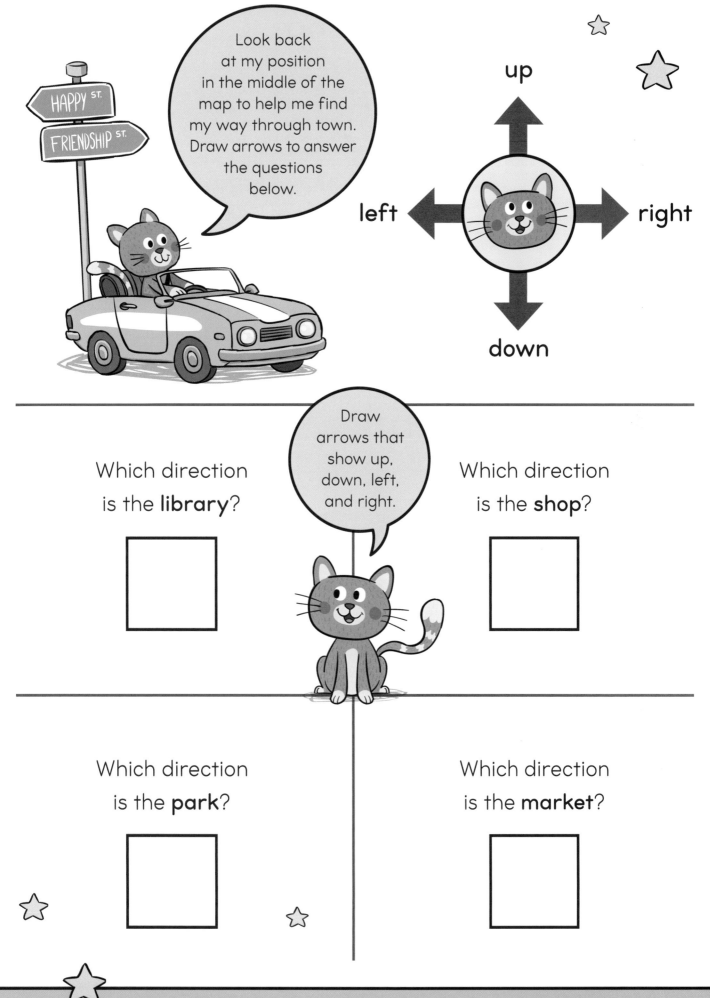

Look back at my position in the middle of the map to help me find my way through town. Draw arrows to answer the questions below.

up

left   right

down

Which direction is the **library**?

Draw arrows that show up, down, left, and right.

Which direction is the **shop**?

Which direction is the **park**?

Which direction is the **market**?

HAPPY ST.

FRIENDSHIP ST.

At Camp

Everyone is at **Camp Happy Town**!
Circle the picture that best describes each statement.

Pig is **on**
the bridge.

Dog is **in front of**
the mountain.

Ant is **next to** the tent.

Iguana is **under** the umbrella.

The sleepy campers are **in** the tent.

Penguin is **behind** the tree.

Wren is **above** the pond.

My Family

All **families** are different!
Draw or write answers to the questions.

This is my family:

There are

_____

people in
my family.

Who is
in your
family?

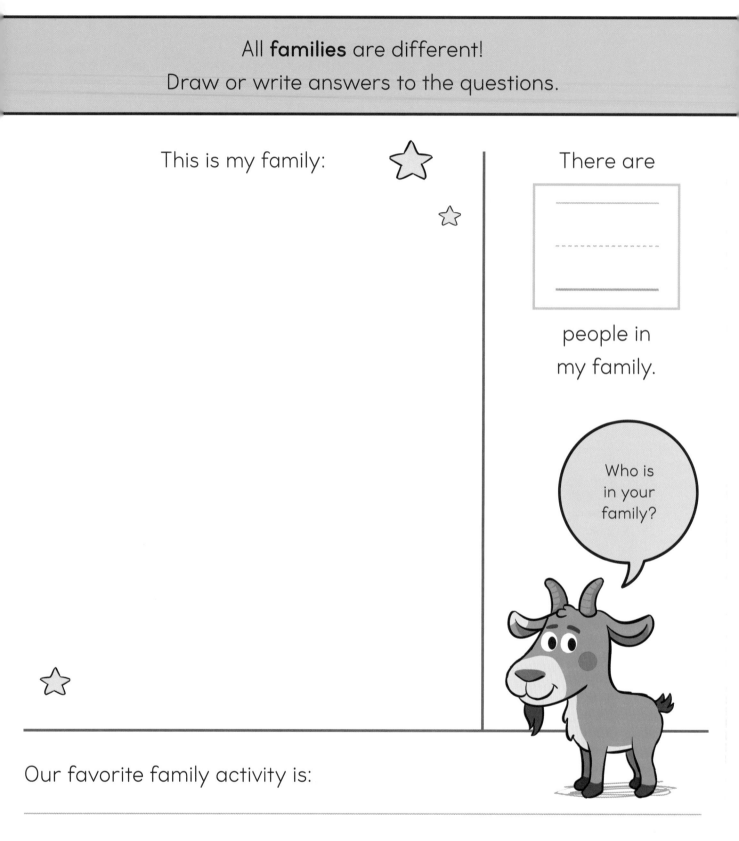

Our favorite family activity is:

_____

_____

About Me

My name is:

_____

Draw a picture of yourself here:

I am

years old.

Answers

READING AND WRITING

Page 10:
ant: Aa
bee: Bb
cat: Cc
dog: Dg
elephant: Ee

Page 11:
frog: Ff
goat: Gg
hippo: Hh
iguana: Ii
jaguar: Jj
kangaroo: Kk
lion: Ll

Page 12:
mouse: Mm
newt: Nn
octopus: Oo
polar bear: Pp
quail: Qq
rabbit: Rr
snake: Ss

Page 13:
tiger: Tt
unicorn: Uu
vulture: Vv
walrus: Ww
X-ray fish: Xx
yeti: Yy
zebra: Zz

Page 14:
zoo
dog
key
ant
egg
bus

Page 15:
Match: tub, u
Match: map, a

Match: hog, o
Match: pig, i
Match: hen, e

Page 16:
Circle: x; fox
Circle: t; hat
Circle: n; sun
Circle: b; web
Circle: g; frog

Page 17:
pen
mop
cup
bag
net
pan

Page 18:
cat, hat
van, pan
pig, dig
dog, log

Page 19:
hen, pen
mop, hop
rug, bug
fox, box
up, cup

Page 20:

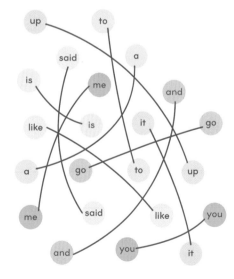

Page 21:

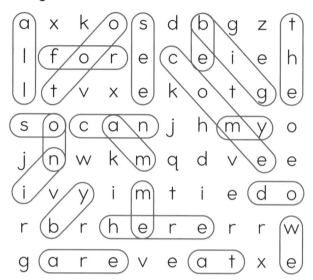

Page 24:
dog: color 1 dot
butterfly: color 3 dots
egg: color 1 dot
flower: color 2 dots
book: color 1 dot
alpaca: color 3 dots

Page 25:
Match: frog, 1; box, 1
Match: octopus, 3; unicorn, 3
Match: zebra, 2; rabbit, 2

Page 26:
Cat drives a car.
Dog is on the log.

Page 27:
Bee reads a book.
Lion goes to the library.

Pages 28-29:

MATH

Pages 32:
Match: 1, boat, one
Match: 2, party hats, two
Match: 3, bananas, three
Match: 4, pens, four
Match: 5, shells, five
Match: 6, oranges, six
Match: 7, apples, seven
Match: 8, beach balls, eight
Match: 9, ice-cream cones, nine
Match: 10, fish, ten

Page 33:
Match: 11, balloons, eleven
Match: 12, gifts, twelve
Match: 13, suns, thirteen
Match: 14, carrots, fourteen
Match: 15, hats, fifteen
Match: 16, logs, sixteen
Match: 17, soccer balls, seventeen
Match: 18, crowns, eighteen
Match: 19, footballs, nineteen
Match: 20, flowers, twenty

Page 34:
1, 3, 5, 7
5, 10, 15, 20
10, 12, 14, 16

Page 35:
party hats, 2, even
pens, 4, even
gifts, 12, even
apples, 7, odd

Page 36:	**Page 38:**
5	8
20	5
20	4

Page 37:	**Page 39:**
10	7
16	15
12	3
10	1
15	8

Page 40:
pentagon: 5 sides, 5 corners
octagon: 8 sides, 8 corners
rectangle: 4 sides, 4 corners
circle: 1 side, 0 corners

Page 41:
triangle: 3 sides, 3 corners
oval: 1 side, 0 corners
diamond: 4 sides, 4 corners
hexagon: 6 sides, 6 corners

Pages 42-43:

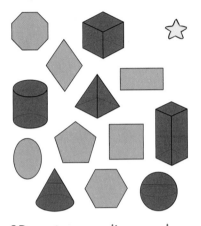

2D: octagon, diamond, rectangle, pentagon, square, oval, hexagon
3D: cube, cylinder, pyramid, cuboid, cone, sphere

Page 44:
Circle: banana; apple; orange
Circle: cup; pen; book
Circle: 2 triangles

Page 45:
Circle: pyramid; cylinder; cube
Circle: second rabbit
Circle: vase; bus; sun
Circle: 8; 12; 16

Page 46:
Circle: giraffe
Circle: elephant
Circle: bird

Page 47:
Circle: bug
Circle: 15cm ruler
Circle: yak
Circle: kite

SCIENCE

Page 48:
Circle: elephant; eagle; boy; mouse; tree; bee; butterfly; cat; bug; flower

Page 49:
Match: mouse, cheese
Match: dog, dog food
Match: monkey, banana
Match: sheep, grass
Match: rabbit, carrots
Match: squirrel, acorn

Page 50:
Match: dog, kennel
Match: rabbit, burrow
Match: fish, pond
Match: bird, nest

Page 51:
caterpillar: 2
cocoon: 3
butterfly: 4

Page 52:

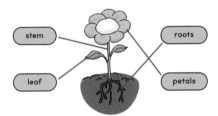

Page 53:
seed: 1
sprout: 2
plant: 3
flower: 4

Page 54:

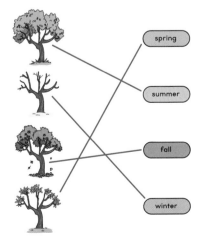

Page 55:

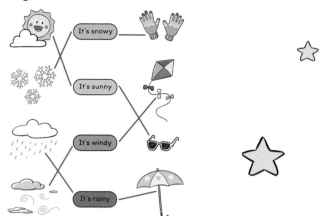

Pages 56-57:

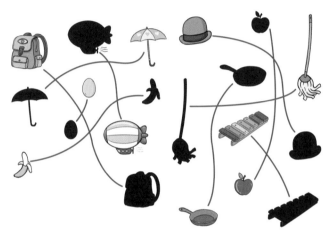

Page 58:
Hot: fire; sun; barbecue
Cold: ice-cream cone; igloo; snowflakes
Page 59:
Solids: bell; newspaper; ball; cake
Liquids: rain; juice; pond

EVERYDAY SKILLS
Page 60:

10 o'clock
6 o'clock
1 o'clock
4 o'clock

Page 61:
12 o'clock
3 o'clock
11 o'clock
8 o'clock
5 o'clock
9 o'clock

Page 62:
Get home from school: afternoon
Go to bed: evening
Wake up: morning
Eat breakfast: morning
Take a bath: evening
See the moon: evening
Page 64:
Tuesday; Thursday; Wednesday
Page 65:
12 months

SOCIAL STUDIES
Page 66:
Healthy: berries; lettuce; apple; banana; orange
Treats: cake; ice-cream cone; milkshake; chips; pie
Page 67:
Circle: jumping rope; running; playing catch; swimming
Page 68:
chips: 2 nickels
milk: 2 dimes and 1 penny
yo-yo: 2 dimes and 1 nickel
Page 69:
Match: plastic bottle, plastic bin
Match: newspaper, paper bin
Match: jar, glass bin
Match: can, metal bin
Pages 70-71:
library: left; shop: down; park: up; market: right
Pages 72-73:

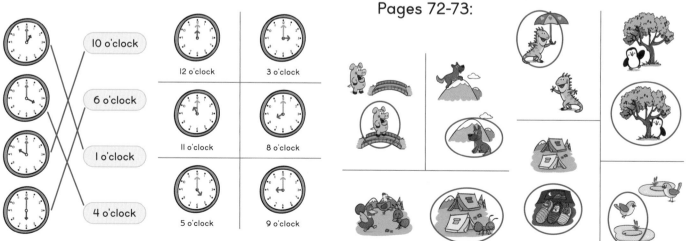

Certificate

This certificate is awarded to:

for learning kindergarten basic skills!

Age: _____ Date: _____

Signed: _____

THE READING HOUSE

STAR OF THE WEEK